What You Need To Know Didn't Know Or Were Afraid To Ask

About Funeral Arrangements, Preplanning, and the Process That Occurs After A Death

Sharon Mitchell

authorHOUSE®

AuthorHouse™
1663 Liberty Drive
Bloomington, IN 47403
www.authorhouse.com
Phone: 1-800-839-8640

First published by AuthorHouse 4/28/2011

ISBN: 978-1-4567-4088-7 (e)
ISBN: 978-1-4567-4089-4 (sc)

Library of Congress Control Number: 2011902395
Printed in the United States of America

I have talked with a multitude of people at probably the worst time of their lives. I am a funeral director and embalmer. The range of emotions a person goes through can span the entire spectrum of emotions. There is a job that needs to be done. It does not matter if the person handling it for the family is demonstrative or passive. Like all professions, one must master a specific art in order to handle certain situations. Every situation is unique. This book will cover what everyone that is handling a loved one's service needs to know. There are specific processes that one needs to have a working knowledge of in order to be able to handle the loved ones service. These are hard decisions that need to be met with grace. Not every situation will have a truthful person handling it. It may be due to lack of knowledge or someone trying to take shortcuts to end an unpleasant task. I do not think any of us want to be the one to handle the end process. However, if we have some knowledge it will certainly go better for us.

One thing I have learned is the art of listening. I have heard in the majority of these meetings, "I have no idea what the funeral or death process involves or what I am supposed to do." Then, there may also be family disagreements that add to the confusion. If you are fortunate, you will find a funeral director who will take the time, care and the commitment you deserve in guiding you through this process. If you do not, then perhaps, I can offer you some comfort and incite as to what you will need. This book is a must read for anyone who will go through this process. Flip through the pages for incite on all topics, death related.

Remember, you deserve all of the very best care, integrity and service possible. We, as funeral directors, will never experience the extreme pain and confusion that you do. Nevertheless, we can assist you in this process and make our part in this at least ease some of the pain and worries while you navigate through the death process.

None of us will ever truly comprehend death, but you can count on the finality that death will affect all of us. As long as life is present, so must death be present. Death is inevitable, that of our own or someone we know or love, and no matter what our station in life is, we will all be touched. We will experience the death of a parent, a spouse, a child, a lover or a friend and eventually we will face our own. The goal of this book and funeral arranging in general, is to make this process a healthier, less stressful and confusing time.

I will give you information and try to answer some questions that you may not have known to ask, will be asked, or were afraid to ever ask. Remember, you can and should ask anything you want to know. There are NO stupid questions. This is one of the major financial expenditures you will make in your life besides the purchase of house or car. Directors are there to serve your needs, just let them.

Chapter I
The Place of Death

The things you need to do when the death occurs will depend on where the death takes place. If it is at a hospital, nursing home, under hospice care, or at another facility, the staff there can help you. You just need to let them know who your funeral home of choice is. If you have not decided, then you have some options before you decide. You can let the deceased be taken to the morgue at the facility if they have one, or have them call a funeral home and have the deceased taken to their facility until you decide on a funeral home you wish to use.

If the death was an accident, or a death that occurred when the person was alone, or if there are suspicious circumstances, the procedures are a bit different. You will need to call the police department or the local law enforcement agency in the area. A Justice of The Peace (a judge) will need to be advised of the death. Usually the police officers will handle this and they will know the jurisdiction and which judge to call. It will be at the discretion of the judge as to whether or not an autopsy will be ordered. If there is to be an autopsy, the judge will decide to which medical examiners office the body will be transported. You will then have time to decide whom you wish the body to be released to after the autopsy has been done. I will take at least 24 hours or more for this to occur depending on the workload and schedule at the coroner or medical examiners office.

If an autopsy is not ordered then the judge will grant permission to have the body removed from the scene of the death. The body will then be moved to a funeral home of the judge's discretion to be held until the family is notified of the death. Then the family can make the decision of where they wish the body to be taken. You DO NOT have to use the funeral home the body was taken. If you do not want to use this funeral home, you are not required to do so. It is your choice, if you change funeral home locations or not, it is your choice. It is ok to choose another funeral home.

The place of death will also be one of the deciding factors as to who will sign the death certificate. It may be a physician, a judge, or a medical examiner. It will depend on the circumstances of the death as to which of these individuals will agree to sign the death certificate. The funeral home will take care of this process. This will be explained in detail for you later in the book.

Chapter 2
Choosing a Funeral Home

The funeral home you choose may be an easy decision if there is only one in the area and you know of one you want to use because of convenience or if your family or friends have used their services in the past. If there are multiple funeral homes to use, then you need to know what is important to you when you make the decision of a funeral home.

Do you want a privately owned or family funeral home versus a corporate owned or conglomerate funeral establishment? It is perfectly acceptable to base your choice on prices and each establishment must provide you with their price list which will help you make the right choice for you or your family circumstances. Check to see which offers a better value, best fits the assets available for the funeral expenses or feels like a place you would want to work with and that offers you the services and options you desire. You need to have a comfort level with the funeral home to which you are intrusting your loved one. It is ok to check out your options if you feel up to it or if you have someone to do it for you. You can visit with a director and see facilities before making your ultimate decision with no obligation or charges.

Think about things that will be important to you and your family. Do you want a funeral home that will handle just the usual funeral services? Or, do you want a full service establishment? All will handle the preparation of the body, funeral arrangements, paperwork, and visitation if desired. There are others funeral homes who will have more services such as flowers, catering, help with travel arrangements, hotels and the like. You can ask each place what they offer or you will see the services listed on their price list. These services may be priced separately or they could be included various packaged selections. The packages may group more items at a discounted price. Your choices will be based on the desires of the deceased, your family desires or the financial circumstances involved and how much you wish to be involved.

There is nothing that states you must spend a lot of money for a funeral, cremation or whatever your choice of disposition is. The amount you spend is not linked in anyway to how much you loved or cared for the deceased. Take time to know what you can afford, what finances you have available to spend, and what the loved one would have wanted. Do not spend money you do not have or cannot get, be realistic. There can be a meaningful and wonderful service for any budget. Just let the funeral director know your constraints and they will help you with decisions and suggestions that will keep you within the guidelines and budget you have in mind as best as they possibly can. There is nothing wrong with stating you only have a certain amount available to work with. Their job is to assist you or advise you on the best way to do this.

Most funeral homes **will** expect payment prior to the date of the service. There are few, if any at all, that will make payment arrangements for extended periods. Many will accept assignment on insurance policies if they are available, have no loans that would exclude the use of them, and are valid, payable policies. What does this mean? Let's say your policy is for 20 thousand dollars and your funeral expenses are $7, 500. If this policy is verified, they will take assignment on only the amount owed for the funeral expenses. You will sign documents for the insurance company to pay the funeral home the exact amount due them. If there are excess funds from the policy, the check for this balance will be made by the insurance company to the beneficiary of the policy. If the policy was for an amount less than the total charges, you will only be responsible for paying the balance the insurance does not cover to the funeral home before the service date or whatever the deadline for payment is at your funeral home of choice. The funeral home will then file the claim for the insurance to be paid to them. Some charge a fee for this service and some do not.

If you had a preneed plan then the same

procedure will occur. The only difference would be that this process would go through the preneed company. The purpose of a prearranged plan will be discussed later in the book if you are not aware of what this is.

Chapter 3
Keeping Policy Information Updated

I want to make some comments to you about the importance of keeping insurance companies updated on changes in you life situation. Where you divorced, remarried, or if the beneficiary of your policy is no longer alive, let the insurance company know who the new beneficiary is. I know you are probably saying it does not matter because I have listed a contingent beneficiary. This detail will make a difference to your family or whoever makes your arrangements. Updates will help avoid undue problems for your survivors at the time of your death. If your spouse was the beneficiary and they have died, the person making the arrangements will have to supply a death certificate proving this to the insurance company and the funeral home. If you have multiple children then all will have to sign paperwork stating that they agree to let this policy be used for funeral payment. If they all do not wish to, then problems could arise. If not all of them are available it could just prolong payment problems. Please try to make changes on documents as changes occur in your life situations.

You would be surprised as to how often these seemingly small details can explode into numerous difficulties for the loved ones remaining. You do not want the wrong person to be the one to benefit from your life insurance policy. I have seen this many times and I do not want you or your family to have this happen to them.

Chapter 4
Information You Will Need to Provide for Arrangements

The first thing you will be asked by the director is the biographical information about the deceased. This information will be requested in order to complete the death certificate.

It is very important that you have correct spellings, dates, locations etc. for this legal document. Make sure you verify the information before you sign off because once it is filed it cannot be changed without amending it and having more costs involved for this change.

For the death certificate, you will need to know the following information:

- Correct legal name of the person. First, middle, and last. Where they a Jr., Sr. etc. What other names have they gone by?
- If female, what was the maiden name
- Sex of the deceased
- Race of the deceased

- Age of deceased
- What is their date of birth
- What is their date of death
- Social Security number
- Where was the place of birth: city, state, country, etc?
- Where they a U.S. citizen
- What was the name of the deceased's father
- What was the maiden name of the deceased's mother
- Where did the death occur: hospital, home, nursing home etc?
- What was the address of this person. Is it within city limits.
- What is the marital status: single, married, divorced, widowed etc.
- If they were married what is the wife's maiden name
- What was the highest education the deceased attained
- Were they ever in the armed forces. A DD214 form will be needed if there will be military honors requested. See the section in the book regarding military service.
- What was their occupation and what type of industry
- Who will be the informant for this information, what is their address, what is their relationship to the deceased
- Will there be a burial, cremation, or body donation
- If burial name of the cemetery and the location

Chapter 5
How Many Death Certificates Will You Need

The number of certified death certificates you get is a personal preference. You can get as many as you want or just the amount you need to take care of business. I can give you some of the reasons why a certified copy is necessary. Certified copies will have a seal and show that it is an original, legal copy. This will be the necessary form needed for most of the things you will need to take care of following a death.

1. Social Security Benefits

If the person was married with a surviving spouse or dependant children they will need a copy for social security. This will get the surviving spouse the $255.00 death benefit. It is a one time thing. If the surviving spouse receives this benefit upon the death of a spouse the children or other survivors will not be able to get it when the other spouse dies. Example, your father dies and all of the children are grown. Your mother, the surviving spouse, will get the death benefit. But, when she dies there will not be another $255 benefit available since there is no surviving spouse or dependent children. You will need a death certificate for surviving dependent children so they can get the social security benefits of the deceased parent until they are of age. Your social security office will guide you through these processes depending on which circumstance applies to you.

2. The Will/Lack of Will for Settling of the Estate of the Deceased

You will need a death certificate to take to your attorney so the estate can be settled and necessary documents can be filed and the affairs of the deceased can be handled.

3. Property
You will need a death certificate for any property, residences, buildings etc that the deceased owned. One will be necessary for all vehicles, farm equipment etc. This will allow you to have the titles to these changed to the appropriate individual.

4. Life Insurance, Accident Policies or Preneed (Death) Policies
You will need a copy for each insurance policy. If they are all with the same company you may get by with fewer. Just be sure to check with the company

upon notifying them as to the death of the policy holder.

5. Bank Accounts

The bank will need to have record of the death to close out accounts or change to the name of the surviving individual that may be on the account with the deceased. If the assets are frozen upon a death it is still possible to get money out of these accounts to pay for the funeral bill. You will need to take a copy of the funeral bill to the bank and most times the funds can be made to the funeral home to directly take care of the death charges. The other bills may have to wait until the settling of the estate or whatever the banks and/or attorneys require. Just ask them what is necessary and you will get their guidance.

6. Retirement Funds, Securities, IRAs, Bonds, Certificates of Deposits

Each individual place will require their own death certificate. You may luck out if these are at the same institution. It will depend on their procedures.

7. Credit Cards, Utilities, Medical Bills etc.

Some times you can get by with copies. You should check with the individual places. It is always a good idea to have extra certified copies for just these types of things.

8. Personal Use, Records Keeping

Some people like to just keep a copy for their

own reasons whether it is for a keepsake, future findings, or to just complete their records.

9. Military Pensions or Benefits

You will need to provide proof of death to the military liaison in order to see what benefits you are eligible for after the veteran's death.

10. Miscellaneous

You will know the lifestyle of your loved one better than anyone else so you can decide how many will be necessary. You may enlist the help of your attorney if you cannot decide from the examples given above.

The cost of death certificates may vary from state to state. I will give you the example using Texas prices since this is my state of practice.

The charge for death certificates in Texas are as follows, the first death certificate will cost $21.00 and each one after that will cost $4.00. Example: If you ordered 10 death certificates it would cost you $57.00. This is 21 + (4x9) 36.00. You can always go back and get more death certificates but the state will start over with charges of 21 + whatever number more you need. It is always better to get a few extra at the 4.00 cost.

Chapter 6
Power of Attorney

Many of the families I spoke with during my funeral arrangement conferences did not know that a power of attorney ends upon the death of an individual. Once a person dies, the will or law of intestacy will govern the handling of the deceased estate. Most importantly the power of attorney does NOT take the place or is it in anyway a substitute for a will. Please make sure you have a will or instructions on how you want your estate to be handled after your death. Have your affairs in order prior if at all possible and it will make things much easier upon your death. It is important to have legal counsel in deciding what is the best way to handle this for you or your family.

Chapter 7
Military Veteran Information

You have an option of having military honors for the deceased no matter what type of service you will have. The funeral director will ask you the appropriate questions needed depending on whether it is a burial, cremation or whatever is necessary for the type or arrangements you wish to have.

To secure any honors you will need to provide the funeral home with a discharge document called a DD214. It is the document that states some of the following information of the military service of an individual upon release from the military duty. It will state their name, rank, place of entry into service, place of discharge, what their job was, the places they served, if any honors or medals were received, and other related information. This will be necessary on all branches of the service. The funeral director will have to fax this to the branch they are requesting honors from to show proof of military service and that the discharge from military service was honorable.

What do you get? Each veteran is entitled to receive a flag, the playing of taps, a monument or niche for the place of interment, a military detail to fold and present the flag to the designated individual, and any burial benefits that they may qualify to receive. The ability of a gun volley at graveside will depend on availability or the detail and if the deceased is qualified to receive this honor. Your funeral home can provide you with this information. The benefits will depend on circumstances or status at time of service, such as whether or not they are active, inactive, retired, a former prisoner of war, etc. The funeral home will usually file for all benefits and the veteran's affairs office will respond to the family as to whether or not they qualify.

Flag

The funeral home will secure a flag for the veteran. It will be presented to the spouse or designated person chosen by the surviving family. It can be folded in a triangle and placed on or in the casket or it can be placed on a table or the like for a memorial service. You can still have honors even if the form of disposition chosen is not a burial.

If there is a casket you will need to decide if you want the flag draped on the casket or if you are folding it and placing it inside. If you choose the casket to be draped you will NOT be able to have flowers or any other object on the flag. Your family flowers will need to be standing sprays that will flank the sides of the casket.

Military Monuments & Niche Plaques

Each veteran is entitled to receive either a bronze or granite marker for their grave. These will have their name, rank, branch of service, era of service (such as WWI, WWII, Korea, Vietnam, Desert Storm, through current times, etc), date of birth, date of death and any distinguished medal or honors received by the veteran during military service. The funeral home will have pictures or samples of these so you may make your desired choices. If the deceased will be entombed then a niche will be available depending of the location, such as a mausoleum, columbarium or the like.

Military Detail

If scheduling of the honor guards of the requested branch of service permits each veteran will get a two person detail. They will fold the flag and present it to the person designated by the family and play taps.

A full detail is not available unless the veteran was active duty, retired, a prisoner of war or other required criteria is met. The funeral home will get the information on what will be available to the deceased.

There is a chance to have a VFW detail there as well if the area has an active team to provide this. Again, the funeral home can secure them for you or you can ask them to check into this for you. In the area I worked, we had a wonderful VFW group to do this and they provided the gun salute for all veterans. They were present along with the two person detail from the appropriate branch. It will just depend on your area and what is available.

If you do get a gun salute, the detail will also present the spent shells from the volley. These are usually placed in the folds of the flag. It is a very moving and special tradition.

Chapter 8
Choices of Disposition

As horrifying and harsh as it may be, disposing of the deceased is a task we must all perform or make a decision on. Some of factors that come into play in this decision may include religious or traditional preferences of the deceased and the family, monetary issues, causes of the death, and many more.

Some of the choices available are burial, cremation, or donation for research and education.

If you are not sure what you wish, just talk with the funeral director and let them know some information and they can give you answers that will help you make a decision. If you have issues regarding the different types of disposition, you may want to let your family know in advance. This will help them in making your final arrangements that best suite your desires and beliefs.

Embalming

What is Embalming? Will embalming need to be done?

Embalming is the process or art of preserving the human body by use of chemicals. Intravenous injections are done to delay the normal bodily process of breaking down or decomposing. Blood and body fluids are removed through the venous system and replaced with chemicals through the arterial system. It started with the Egyptians and has evolved through time. Embalming helps to preserve the tissues, maintain color of the body, and restore cosmetic appearances. This is normally done through incisions in major arteries of the body either in the neck, legs or arms. It prevents the spread of diseases, slows the normal breakdown of tissues and provides a temporary preservation of the body to extend the time for the body to present for viewing, visitation, or services. This is just a brief explanation of the process to help you understand and make decisions accordingly.

If it is important to you that the body be viewed and present at services embalming would be necessary. I know some families are concerned that maybe they should not have an open casket because of trauma or an extended illness or other factors are involved. If it is important to have the body viewed and you have concerns, share them with the funeral director.

They are the ones who have seen the body, know the circumstances involved in the death and can talk about what the results embalming can do for appearance. I have heard so many times after embalming that they are so pleased with the results; the loved ones look like they used to before the death or even better than they have for quite some time. There are many gifted embalmers with abilities to make a wonderful outcome that will provide you with the last good memory of the person and an opportunity for a positive closure. If in doubt, let them try and you can make the decision afterward as to whether you want the casket opened or closed. You just may be surprised at the results. The final decision is always yours.

You will need to decide if there will be a service and a visitation with the body present. Will the casket be opened or closed? Will the burial occur within a few days, within 24 hours as some religious practices or personal preferences indicate, or will it be postponed to coordinate with family circumstances. This will dictate what preparation must be done for the deceased and if embalming needs to be done. The funeral director will tell you what needs to be done depending on the choices you make for the services and your time frame of the services.

You **do not** have to be embalmed in the state of Texas. No matter what state you are in, you can find out as to what your state requires through the funeral home you are working with. If you bury within a certain period of time, if the casket is closed or if the body is not present at the services, embalming is not required. If you do not wish the deceased to be embalmed you will need to choose the options for services that take this into consideration. Can the body be refrigerated until the time of disposition, what is the time constraints before disposition, what exactly do you want, and will the body be shipped out of the state or country? Time factors and your choices will dictate the need to embalm or not.

Burial

The choice of ground burial will require that you acquire a cemetery plot. Most likely you will have to get a casket or some type of burial container which will depend on the requirements of the cemetery you choose or if other traditions or religious preferences call for something different. (There will be another section in this book to discuss some examples of some of the things cemeteries may require and what charges may be involved.) There will be charges involved in the opening and closing of the grave.

Cremation

Cremation is the process where the body is enclosed in a container of card board, fiber board or wood. It is placed in a chamber called a retort where open flames rise to a temperature between 1800 to 2400 degrees Fahrenheit for a period of 1.5 to 3 hours. The time will vary with the size of the body and whatever container is used. The water in the body and the soft tissues are consumed by combustion and the afterburner completes the burning process. The cremation remains are cooled and are removed for processing. This involves removing any foreign objects with a magnet or by other means, such as any metal, screws from previous medical procedures, or prosthesis. These are then disposed of according to regulations and policies of the crematory. The remains are then collected, ground up or pulverized into a course powder like state. They are then placed into a temporary container, the vessel or urn of your choice.

Cremation remains may be kept, buried, scattered or interred in a columbarium, made into jewelry, placed in a reef, and many others. If you wish to travel by air with the cremation remains to another location you will need to have the cremation certificate available and check with the airline carrier that you will be using so you will know what their policies require.

Body Donation

If donation is the wish of the family or deceased, you will need to notify the school or facility that you may want the donation to be made to. There should be no preparations done such as embalming prior to contacting them after the death. They will have requirements that need to be met and will tell you whether or not the donation is possible and what steps need to be taken at that time. It may be that the body will be cremated after a period of time when research is completed and then returned to the family. Ask any questions you have regarding the procedures before, during and after the donation. The funeral home may be able to provide you with contacts if needed. Talk about body return. Inquire about the things that happen to the body etc.

Understand what tissue and bone donation entail if you allow this to be done.

You may be asked by groups at a medical facility about the possibility of partial body donation. They may request donation of specific body parts such as bone, tissue, eyes, inner ear etc. When approached, ask questions if you do not understand about the type of donation that is being requested. How will it affect the body is you plan an open casket service? Make sure you have a comfort level and understanding. Is this something important to the deceased or your family? Was the deceased a donor on their drivers' license? Donation is a wonderful thing but may not be right for others. The ultimate decision will be up to you, the deceased wishes, or family choices.

Chapter 9
Types of Funeral Services

After the biographical information is obtained you will be asked to select the type of service you wish to have. You can have a traditional funeral, a graveside service, direct burial or cremation, or a memorial service. If you are not aware of what each may entail I will provide you with a brief explanation of each. If you have other wishes, you can discuss them with the funeral director and they will advise you if it is possible or not.

Traditional Service

This is the type of service where the body is present, with the casket being either opened or closed. It can be a funeral chapel service, a church service or other venue of choice. You will select a clergy person, or some other person to be in charge of the service, the eulogy and the order of the service. You will need to decide if you would like a visitation or some type of prayer service the evening before or at another time before the actual funeral service is conducted. The director can advise you and assist you once your decision is made.

Direct Burial

Direct burial is when the deceased is buried prior to any funeral services taking place, if no services are planned, or if a memorial service of some type will be scheduled at a later time. If direct burial is your choice, remember you not required to have embalming performed. Your funeral director will let you know if any time constraints are involved and if any preparation is required.

Memorial Service

A memorial service is done if burial or cremation has already occurred. The only difference between a memorial service and a traditional service is that the deceased actual body is not present. It can be at any location, a church, funeral home or any other venue that the family wishes. You can have the funeral home take care of all of the paperwork for the death certificate and disposition and have the memorial service on your own. The funeral home can also offer wonderful options on the types of memorial services they can provide. It will be whatever your preference and time frame is. One of the good things about the memorial service is that you can schedule it immediately, at a future time, or whenever you want and at any location you wish.

It can include a clergy person, a formal church service, a party, or an informal service. A memorial service can be personalized to the individual with pictures, videos and much more. Your imagination is your limit, whether on a budget or if extravagance is your desire. It can and should provide a celebration of the life of and honor to the deceased and an occasion for closure for the family.

Graveside Services

The services for the deceased are all conducted at the graveside. The funeral home will make arrangements for the area to be set up with a tent and chairs or whatever the family requires. The body will be taken to this site usually an hour before service time. Any flowers or tributes will be already set up before the family and friends arrive. The service will take place, including any military honors, music may be played or performed live, and it will proceed as any other service would have with the exception that is at graveside and not at a church, funeral home or other location. It can be simple or it can be elaborately planned.

Chapter 10
Type of Clothing Needed

The clothing usually requested by the funeral home will include whatever you want the deceased to wear such as a dress, a suit, jeans, either casual or dress clothes, underwear, socks, booties, or the like, with shoes being optional. I would always tell my families to dress the deceased as they would have wanted. If they never wore dress clothes and suits, do not dress them as such unless it is a family desire. I have buried people with formal wear, casual clothes such as jeans, overalls and shorts, uniforms, and more. The choice is yours and there is no right or wrong decision. The deceased is completely dressed both top and bottom. You would be surprised at how many times families only thought that they had to bring clothes for the upper body. If you have any doubts about what you need to bring, your director is the one to ask.

Most of the time the funeral home will handle

dressing of the deceased but you can request it to be done by someone else if religious preference or family, friends wish to have this honor. Just check with your funeral home and they will try to accommodate as needed.

Hair Decisions

You will need to bring a photo or let the funeral director know how the deceased fixed their hair. This includes not only the style, but also what side the hair is parted on, what if any products the deceased used, will they need to be clean shaven, if not, what will need to be done or what facial hair should remain. Some funeral homes bring in a hairdresser or style the hair but there is nothing wrong with you specifying if a certain stylist is required or desired or if the a family member or a friend wishes to do this.

Make Up

The appearance of the deceased is a top priority to all directors. They will use experience and training to provide the best possible appearance of your loved one. Certain circumstances may require touch up and use of cosmetics. They will always let you approve any work done prior to anyone else viewing the deceased. Let them know ahead of time or bring makeup if there is a specific type the deceased always used. Advise the director if the person wore a little, none or heavy makeup. The goal is to present the deceased in the most natural state that were in during life. If you feel something is not right, not the right shade or whatever, bring it to their attention. They will make adjustments accordingly or explain the reason it has been done a certain way. It is important that you have the best last image of your loved one that you possibly can. We will not know unless you tell us.

Jewelry or Personal Items

The funeral director will ask you if there will be any jewelry or personal items on the deceased and if these items will need to be removed before burial or disposition. If you want an item back you need to advise before interment or entombment occurs. You can leave the items you wish and have them remove others. Will the wedding ring, other rings, earrings, bracelets, medals, pins etc. remain or will they be removed. If yes, to whom shall they be returned to? The same applies to photos and other memorabilia.

You can put anything you wish in the casket with the deceased. Bring these items to the director and let them know where you would like them located. Will it be in a pocket, in their hands, in an area that is visible to all or in a discrete location? Please advise of any particular wishes that you may have.

The director will let you know if there are any problems with your requests.

Chapter 11
Who Will Preside At Services

This is strictly a preference of the family and you will need to let the director know your decisions. Will this person be a clergy person, friend, family member or do you want the funeral home to secure the services of a clergy person if you do not have one in mind or were not part of a church. They always have lists of ministers who are available and can meet with you to get to know your family and particulars about the deceased. Just let the director know the denomination you prefer or what type of personality you prefer. They will try to match the best possible person to meet your criteria.

Chapter 12
Choosing A Casket

There are many types of caskets and price ranges to choose from. During the arrangements the funeral home will show you what they have available or will be able to get to match your needs and desires. Many people choose to have the casket of choice be purchased from the internet, casket store, or have one specially made and delivered to the funeral home. You will need to keep in mind the date and time you have scheduled for the services so know if your preferences or wishes will be possible to accommodate. If there are special circumstances due to religion or personal preference, discuss this with the director prior to making a decision.

Wood

Wood caskets can be made of almost any type of wood. Your funeral home will carry a variety which can include pecan, cherry, oak, maple, pine, mahogany, poplar and other hardwoods. Wood caskets are porous and will not be gasketed or locking the same as some metal or steel casket would.

Various Metal Caskets

There is a wide variety of choices which include Bronze, Copper, stainless steel, regular steel caskets. This will be based on the gauge of the metal such as 20, 18, 16, 14 etc. The lower the gauge the higher the quality of the metal and therefore a price consideration.

There are beautiful colors and styles in all price ranges. Your consideration or choices can be based on any number of factors such as your personal preferences or those of the deceased, style, what looks best with what you want the deceased to wear, the size of casket best meets the needs of the deceased, your financial constraints as well as others. The casket is just the frame, the art is your loved one so make a choice that will meet all of your needs and not cause financial burdens or regrets. The price has no bearing on how much you loved or how you felt about the deceased. Be practical and follow good judgment. You should only be concerned about your preferences and budget. Do not care about what anyone else will think or the opinions they have, it has to be the right choice for you and your loved ones.

Other Materials

There a caskets of fiberboard covered with various cloth material, laminates, cremation caskets, and cremation boxes that one can choose from. These choices can be based on many criteria such as cost considerations, desire for biodegradable or green material, and many other personal reasons. Again, the only consideration should be your desires and the stipulations under which you and your family must work.

All of the choices can still have the same outcome, a wonderful tribute and celebration for the deceased and your family. The funeral home will be happy to assist you and address any questions or concerns that you may have or may encounter.

Casket Sizes

There are times when specialized caskets are needed. There are oversized or larger caskets available to accommodate larger individuals or uncommonly tall individuals. If in doubt or have concerns about the casket size, voice your concerns during arrangements. Remember both you and the funeral home want to present the best possible presentation of the deceased. You want a good combination of fit and comfort appeal for the deceased during viewing.

Chapter 13
Urns

Urns options will include wood, ceramic, metal, biodegradable products, chimes, sundials, jewelry, and just about anything else you can think of.

You can have an urn hand made by a loved one or craftsman of your choice.

There are many types of containers and vessels that are suited for this purpose. Your choices and ideas can be your guide in choosing just the right option for your needs.

Chapter 14
Outer Burial Containers, Liners, and Vaults

A liner is a container that the casket is placed in for burial. It can be made of various materials. In earlier years some liners were made of wood. Since wood is porous and is collapsible this version is not used much, if any, now.

Concrete liners are boxes made of concrete that the casket is placed in prior to burial. Both the bottom and top or lid of this type is made of concrete. Many cemeteries that require outer burial containers will use this concrete version as the minimal acceptable kind. This is a container that is porous and therefore will allow water to enter and exit it. It has holes at the bottom of the base as well. The main purpose of the liner is to hold the load or weight of the dirt placed on the grave. It keeps the casket from crushing due to the dirt placed on top. It can help to keep the grave site from sinking as badly if machinery is used in the cemetery and just from normal climatic situations. It will not protect the casket from elements such as water, air, bugs and other such factors.

A polygard or hard plastic like material can be used. This is stronger than a concrete liner. Most of the time they will have a dome shaped lid that will help to shed water. It does keep out more elements than just a concrete or wood liner would. It too holds the weight of the dirt to prevent damage to the casket such as crushing, grave sinking in the like.

Your funeral home will have small versions of the types they offer and will be glad to explain the value or qualities of the choices.

Vaults

There are many varieties of these and many different brands. They can be made of a combination of various materials and concrete. They are the best protection you can get to encase and protect the casket. It holds the weight of the dirt and keeps out many elements such as air, water, dirt, insects etc. that liners would not. It is usually set up at the graveside with its own lowering device due to its weight. It will be slightly visible at the gravesite prior to burial. The lid is on a devise to the side of the casket. After services, the bottom of the vault will be raised to completely encase the casket. The device to the side will then place the lid over the bottom of the base. This will form at type of seal and the entire unit will then be lowered into the grave and the grave will be closed or filled with dirt as usual.

The prices of each individual type will vary depending on the material that it is made of. You can get bronze, copper, stainless steel, and other choices. The cost can range from a couple of thousand to 10,000 or more. The funeral home will have information on the brand they carry and the cost associated with each. They may have small versions of each type in their selection room and/or a photo of how it appears at the gravesite.

The Choice to Purchase or Not Purchase

Your choice of a liner or vault will be a matter of what your preferences are and what the cemetery requires that you are interring at. Many cemeteries do not require a liner or vault. If this is the case then the additional cost of purchasing a liner or vault will be your preference. It may be based on what your family has done for a previously buried loved one. If you do not know or did not discuss this option before, I will give you the same example that I used when meeting with the families that I served.

My father was an ashes to ashes dust to dust believer. We buried him in a wooden casket with no liner or vault straight into the ground. He believed in just letting nature and the elements take their course. He was not concerned about the possibility of the casket crushing due to the weight of the dirt on top. It was a personal preference for him.

My mother on the other hand hates the idea of

any water touching her body and wants to have the ultimate protection of a vault.

There is no right or wrong decision. You can base your choice to purchase or not to purchase on the above examples as well as the financial resources, religious preferences and what the funeral home has available. If cost is a major consideration and your cemetery does not require a liner or vault, do not spend the extra money. Remember it is what is important to you that will be your guide. It does not matter what anyone else thinks and chances are the majority of the people attending will not even notice one way or the other. The only thing that will matter is if the cemetery has restrictions.

Chapter 15
Memorial Folders

The funeral home will offer some selections of memorial folders that you can have for those in attendance at the service. They will vary in design, size, and content depending on the funeral home you choose. They can include a photo of the deceased if you want a more personalized selection.

They usually include the name of the deceased, the place and date of their birth and death, where the services will take place, the name of the cemetery, the pallbearer's names etc.

You will need to check with your church to see if they may provide a bulletin for the service and what it will include. You can then opt to either have the folders with them or not at all. If you like they can be designed and printed by a family member, friend or business. This would be something you would most likely have to arrange for if you do not wish to use what is available through the funeral home. This will be one of the topics discussed in making the funeral arrangements.

Prayer Cards

These are small cards that have a scenic photo, religious figure or scene, as well as other designs on the front. The back will usually state the deceased name, age, date of birth and death. It can also include a bible verse, poem, or prayer of the family's choosing. These can be distributed at the prayer service or visitation prior to the service or at the funeral service.

Its use is based on family or religious preferences.

Chapter 16
Flowers

Casket Spray

You will need flowers for the top of the casket if there will be no flag on the casket. This arrangement is known as a casket spray. Some funeral homes provide this in a package or you can go to your florist of choice and see the different styles available and the costs. These prices will vary depending on the type of flowers desired, the size and of course, the varying florist charges. It can be personalized as you desire with banners which say husband, wife, father, mother or other sentiments and sayings. It can be a traditional piece or a simple single flower.

Family Pieces

These are usually standing sprays or pieces that designate the relation of the sender such as children, grandchildren, brother, sister, uncle, cousin or others.

Boutonnières

These will be the flowers that will be given to the pallbearers, honorary pallbearers or any other group you wish to distinguish at the service.

Sending Flowers For A Service

There is no set standard on the type of flowers whether it is a spray, pot plant, cut flower, or special design piece. It is your gesture and can be the type or variety of your choosing. Keep in mind the price you are willing to pay, the delivery charges involved, and the time of the service. The florist will be able to make suggestions that best suite your desires and price range.

It will matter what kind of flowers you send for a memorial service. It is best if you send cut flowers, pot plants and the like. Standing sprays are a bit of a waste since there will not be a grave site involved and the family usually does not wish to take these arrangements home.

Chapter 17
Memorial Tributes

You can designate that you prefer a memorial be given in lieu of flowers or for those who do not like to send flowers, or as an additional choice for people wishes to express their sympathy. This can be to an already established charity, a church, school, university or college, a scholarship fund, a fund for surviving children or their education or a fund to help with funeral expenses. Funeral homes usually have envelopes to place at the registry for guests or will make appropriate arrangements for the supplying information and envelopes or addresses for the individual one you choose.

Chapter 18
Choosing Pallbearers

The number of pallbearers needed can be anywhere from 6-8 individuals. The number will depend on the size of the body, your preferences, preferences the deceased had requested in prior conversations regarding their services, or other such factors. The group that you designate to actually participate in carrying the casket are called active pallbearers. It does not matter about gender and if the age of the person makes their ability to perform this duty questionable, you can have the others involved carry more of the burden of weight. This will still allow their participation.

Honorary pallbearers are the group you wish to distinguish in a special way due to personal, professional, or for whatever reasons you may have. They may follow behind the active pallbearers, line the path the active pallbearers take, have a special seating area etc. This can be any amount from 1 to

100's depending on the circumstances. You do not have to have honorary pallbearers but it does give you the ability to acknowledge certain individuals in a special way.

Chapter 19
Choosing Music

There is no set rule on music. You can have traditional religious music, soft music, music of a specific era or type, or a selection of music that was the favorite of the deceased or the family in general. If the service is at the funeral home they will honor whatever you wish. There may be some stipulations if a religious ceremony is involved, preferences of the officiate, or the type venue you choose outside of the funeral home facilities. You can advise the officiate of your desires and then discuss if they will be permitted.

Chapter 20
Photos & Other Memorabilia

Family photos depicting the deceased life and family members are always a nice touch at any type of service. They can just be displayed for the time the deceased is lying in state at the funeral home or can go to the place where the services will take place as well. Personalization of services has become a popular part of the funeral process. The funeral home will welcome the display of items such as uniforms, honors, and others. Discuss the items of importance with the director and what options that will be available to you.

Video Tributes

Many funeral homes now offer the service of making a video tribute with photos that the family brings. They will compile these photos into a video presentation with a musical background. If this is not available at your funeral home, they may have a screen and equipment available for the video that you have made and bring in. They can also tell you of places that can possibly make them if this service is not available in house.

Receptions and Catering

Some funeral homes will offer services of using the funeral home for a reception following a service or for a visitation. They may also have in house catering options. Many of the larger or city based funeral homes will offer this service. The funeral director will be able to tell you what they can provide.

Chapter 21
Desired Seating of Family

The director will ask you about your seating preferences. If the services are at the funeral home do you wish to sit in the front of the chapel, in front of the speaker, in an area to the side or with more privacy? They will ask if you wish to be brought in after all are seated or if they wish to just take their seats informally as others. If your services are at a church the same questions will be addressed and information will be given as to how that particular place usually conducts services.

You will need to know how many seats should be reserved. Will it be only enough for immediate family, or will you extend reserved seating for extended family and friends? Do you want everyone on one side or divided a certain way on both sides of the aisle.

Chapter 22
Obituaries

You will need to decide if you will write your own obituary, use one the deceased prepared, or will you provide information and allow the funeral director to write it and have you edit it. It can be short and to the point or it can be extensive. You will need to decide if you wish the obituaries to be published and where or just displayed at the registry at the funeral home and on their website.

Obituary charges have a variety of cost factors. Major newspapers will charge by the letter, the word or inch. There will be a charge to include a photo or verse with the obituary. This can be quite substantial depending on the paper. Be sure to have the funeral home check the costs for the papers you desire and then let you know the charges before submitting for publication.

Hometown newspapers may charge a less

amount, they may print for free if the deceased had ties in the community, or they will edit the obit and print their abbreviated version at no charge. Again, the funeral home will be able to find out the charges before publishing.

Brief Obituaries

Brief obituaries are most often run at no charge, even in the larger papers. This is often submitted by the funeral home for all deceased on an automatic basis when their funeral home is used for arrangements. It will state the name of the deceased, age, place of death, occupation, where, when, and type of services planned and the location of the burial.

If you insist on adding survivors or other personal information, charges will be accrued accordingly.

Chapter 23
Cemetery Information

If you are going to bury, you will need to secure plots at the cemetery of your choice. If you have already made these arrangements the cemetery will still have to be notified of the death and they may request your presence to identify the spots owned and to designate the burial space if multiple spaces are owned. Taking the time to do this will just insure there will be no surprises or mistakes made in the interment process. This will give you an opportunity to find out if outer burial container are required, what type of monuments are allowed and just find out the regulations in general. There will be a set charge for opening and closing of the grave. There could be a charge for marking the grave or securing a deed for the property. The funeral director can arrange certain parts if not all of this for you. You will need to decide if you want a tent, multiple tents, chairs or what other items you may desire or require. The director will need to know if a monument is already in place. If there is one there, will you need the funeral home to get the date of death engraved on the monument or was has arrangements for this already been made?

The same would apply regarding a columbarium, a mausoleum or whatever the type of interment you desire. The director can give you guidance on this.

Chapter 24
Monuments

The type of monument you choose will need to be based first on what is allowed at the cemetery. Some will have restrictions based on their cemetery. You will need to know if the monument must be a flat or if it can be upright, is there a size restriction, is there a material restriction (can it be granite or does it have to be bronze or something different). Some cemeteries require them to be flat due to maintenance issues. It is easier to mow and trim around flat monuments. Are you allowed to have benches, fountains, etc? Always check the cemetery restrictions before spending money on something they will not allow you to place in their cemetery.

There a multitude of materials used to make monuments. Traditionally these are granite, but can be marble, glass, wood, bronze, or the like. Many new ideas and materials are available now then in the past.

There are many designs options regarding size, color, photos, lettering, and much more. Many funeral homes will have books to help you make some choices or get ideas. If there is already a certain type of monument already there for another loved one or family member, you can have a duplicate made to match if desired. Usually monument companies will charge a small fee to match but it can be done fairly easily. Just let your funeral director or monument person know what you wish.

The best thing to do is to make a drawing of what you have in mind and bring it or just tell the person you are discussing the monument with you.

I have helped in drawing a design and then send it to the monument company. They will usually do a computer printout of how it will look and send it to the funeral director for your final approval. Make sure all names are spelled correctly and dates are correct before signing off on the design. What you sign for is what you will get so make sure it is right and no costly mistakes are made.

There can be laser art on the stone depicting scenes, hobbies of the person, various flowers, leaves or whatever you desire. There can be banners, books, squares, scrolls or plain areas on which to place the pertinent information such as name, date of birth, date of death and any verses, poems. Do you wish the name to be on the back of the monument?

The possibilities are endless. The director will be glad to assist you in planning the monument and they will give you ideas or suggestions that you may not have thought of.

They can also assist you with the various finishes that are available such as smooth, rough (balance rock pitch), the different tops that are available and much more. They will make this process easier for you and help you make your final decisions.

Chapter 25
Preplanning Services

You can preplan your services or those of your loved ones in advance of the death. This can be very helpful for many reasons. The individual can participate in the planning and therefore you know exactly how they would like their service to be and what is important to them. It also makes it easier at the time of death because most of the decisions have been made in advance and not at a time of grief and stress.

These can be done several ways. You can just let the funeral home know what you wish and they can have a file stating your preferences. If you just give them the information and not prepay using a preneed company through the funeral home they cannot lock in prices.

If you do formally make a preneed the prices of today will be locked in and will not change at the time of death, whether that is one year or many years from the date of the preneed. Certain things cannot be locked in price wise if the funeral home does not have control of them, such as the cost of death certificates and the like. The prices they control such as merchandise, services, and preparation of the body can be. You can sit down and discuss a preneed with a funeral professional at no obligation.

The prices will be based on your choices of services, merchandise etc.

If you pay in full at the time of the preneed you are pretty much assured all will go easily at the time of death. If you make payments, there could be some charges at the time of death. There is a certain time frame of which one must survive after making a preneed. The paperwork must have had a chance to go through and other factors are taken into consideration by the preneed company. If for example one dies before complete payment is made they will only receive the amount of the premiums that they paid in towards the funeral bill. Depending on your company and their contract the amount of available funds will vary if premature death occurs.

Premium amounts will vary if not paid in full at the time of the preneed. Factors that affect this will be age, how long the payment plan is that is chosen, the type of policy it is, and other things such as these that I have mentioned.

It is still an excellent idea to preplan. It can not only save you money, but will also help to make the funeral planning go easier and free you from making important decisions when you may not be in the best frame of mind and under stress.

Many, or should I say most people, do not wish to discuss death but letting loved ones know your preferences, wishes or desires is vital. It may also help if not all of the survivors are in agreement over what should be done.

If it is preplanned, the decisions have already been made and the process will go easier and avoid possible family disagreements at an already emotionally charged time.

If you are not sure about preplanning, just speak to a funeral director or preneed person and get facts that will help you decide if this is a good option for you and your family. It could make a tremendous difference at time of need.

Chapter 26
Final Comments

I hope that this information will help you make the death process decisions a bit easier. I know there will be many more questions that you may have. I just want you to know that it is okay to ask anything. Let us, as funeral professionals, make this a less stressful time. The life of an individual is truly something to honor and celebrate. We take our jobs very seriously and it is truly an honor to serve you in providing a meaningful and lasting tribute to your loved one. It is the last "good thing" you can do for someone and we are here to offer our talents, insight, and education to make a final tribute to a life that has touched so many and especially to the ones that they loved most---you.